Magick of the Seven Olympian Spirits

S ROB

ISBN:1983819018
ISBN-13:9781983819018

DEDICATION

I dedicate this book to my mother and father.

CONTENTS

ACKNOWLEDGMENTS

I acknowledge the existence of real magick.

Chapter 1

This book is not just another book of magick because it helps us to explore what these Seven Olympian Spirits are. In fact, how we view them is unusual because when people believe something they have some affect over it and so change or manifest into the world what did not exist. However, the Seven Olympian Spirits are linked to planets and so could be viewed as sky gods. But they are also thought of as being demonic and often through that it is best to summon them alongside seven particular Angels: so that the light and the dark are used at the same time. But the seven Olympic spirits are not fallen angels, and so should be thought of as being merely demonic and so less than the devils. But in truth this is simply not the case they are extremely powerful and so this seems to indicate that they are just what they are said to be spirits, entities outside of the system of good and evil: but who usually seem to have chosen the demonic as being their side. But is this so unusual when in fact much of what is said to be considered bad through study of religion seems often to harm no one? The seven Olympic spirits are sometimes named the seven Alchemists and this is perhaps a better description but I will use the Seven Olympian Spirits terminology because it is the most recognised.

However, if we look at the hierarchy of angels and of devils we notice that at higher levels much of what occurs through angels is about the actual controlling of the universe: so that everything keeps going. But this is not present in the hierarchy of devils and so this is done mainly through the Olympian spirits. This means that they must represent the demonic insofar as controlling of the universe and reality goes. This also means that the higher-level angels and the Olympic spirits are essentially doing the same job. This also means that the Seven Olympian Spirits really are the occultism that gives the universe balance and so without them no freewill would be possible. The Seven Olympian Spirits are all great occultists and yet although they seem to stand on the side of the demonic, this is because without it everything would fall: they are the lynchpin which keep reality, thought and freedom of choice in place. This means that they could quite easily take control and yet do not because it is unnecessary, because being the lynchpin of everything and being really neither completely good nor bad and after all the world and reality is neither good or bad also: but both.

But this also follows with the high angelic beings and if we look closely we find many things there that may appear to us also, as not being completely good or bad. This is not so strange when we consider that in occultism there are many forces and entities of a magical nature that exist outside of good versus evil and that most of these are like us; more than similar to any ideal. The Seven Olympic Spirits are named Aratron, Bethor, Phaleg, Och, Hagith, Ophiel and Phul and they are all different with different powers. However, to summon them you will be utilising the Roman god Janus and he is a god with two faces: one looks towards the future and the other the past and he control gateways and doorways. This does mean that he can open a gateway through which any of the Seven Olympian Spirits may pass through into our world. They will then be commanded and sent back through the gateway: which Janus will close again. You may wonder how you a mere human can command any of the Olympic Spirits or Janus and the reason is simple, we humans possess a powerful will and this coupled with the correct methods can get even the strongest of magical beings to do our bidding. In fact, it is better to think of these beings as magical beings, rather than deities. This means that this magick is about bringing humanity to a higher level and more powerful position. However, I do know that this magick here will seem strange to some, but the only real reason that this is so, is that when you give it real thought, it actually leads to a more complicated arrangement: but one not unlike ours on the Earth.

I will not talk about Aratron and he is the first of the Olympian spirits, he is an alchemist and commands seventeen million six hundred and forty thousand spirits. Aratron is linked to Saturn and he rules forty-nine provinces. Aratron has power over transmutation: but like all Olympian spirits it is better to simply think of his power as being magick itself. The first magick you will learn will be simply for Aratron to empower you: give you great power. But as power is always useful to use, this magick does make sense and so here is this magick now: will it to work and it shall.

Aratron for great power

Janus god of great power, you have two faces and while one of your faces always looks towards the future, one always looks towards the past. Janus, you control the gateway and I ask that you open the gates so that the way through to the Olympian spirits is open, the way through to the seven Alchemists. Janus open the gateway, open the gates here and now: Janus opens the gateway the gateway is open. Aratron first of the Olympian spirits, great alchemist, ruler of forty-nine provinces, he of Saturn and who may call on seventeen million six hundred and forty thousand spirits. Aratron step through the gateway and be here with me: Aratron step through the gates and be here with me. Aratron step through the gates; Aratron steps through the gates and is here with me. Aratron you are a great alchemist and transformation and all magick are yours to control and I ask that you give me greater power, make greater power mine and this is what I ask of you. Aratron agrees to help and departs back through the gates. Janus god of great power, you have two faces and while one of your faces always looks towards the future, one always looks towards the past. Janus, you control the gateway and I ask that you close the gates. Janus close the gateway, close the gates here and now: Janus closes the gateway the gateway is shut. So it is and will be.

If you worked that last magick it is quite possible that you saw, felt, sensed or heard Aratron and maybe also Janus. If this is in fact what happened, then that is brilliant but it is often the case that people that people need time for them to be seen. But in fact, most people do feel a change of temperature when they are present and this is physical proof of their presence. But in fact, the true proof is the affect this magick has on your life and this means that you should not choose to not be powerful because doing this, is being powerless. This means that when this magick gives you opportunities for power: which you think are good opportunities: then take them, do not live in regret but do what you can. But here is some magick to become richer because through its power, wealth in all forms can be drawn to you.

Aratron to attract wealth

Janus god of great power, you have two faces and while one of your faces always looks towards the future, one always looks towards the past. Janus, you control the gateway and I ask that you open the gates so that the way through to the Olympian spirits is open, the way through to the seven Alchemists. Janus open the gateway, open the gates here and now: Janus opens the gateway the gateway is open. Aratron first of the Olympian spirits, great alchemist, ruler of forty-nine provinces, he of Saturn and who may call on seventeen million six hundred and forty thousand spirits. Aratron step through the gateway and be here with me: Aratron step through the gates and be here with me. Aratron step through the gates; Aratron steps through the gates and is here with me. Aratron you are a great alchemist and transformation and all magick are yours to control and I ask that you attract wealth to me, let wealth flow to me that will become mine and this is what I ask of you. Aratron agrees to help and departs back through the gates. Janus god of great power, you have two faces and while one of your faces always looks towards the future, one always looks towards the past. Janus, you control the gateway and I ask that you close the gates. Janus close the gateway, close the gates here and now: Janus closes the gateway the gateway is shut. So it is and will be.

The magick you have learnt in this chapter is not just powerful but helpful. Through the power of Aratron you will find that your life will be transformed: but also, so may you. This is because through him the truth of the world and a greater more powerful path can be revealed. Use this magick while willing it to work and Aratron will always be with you when you work the magick.

Chapter 2

I will now talk about the second of the Seven Olympian Spirits and his name is Bethor. Bethor has great wisdom and is a healer and can bestow very long life and he can give great wealth; being also an alchemist and he is linked to Jupiter. Bethor also can command twenty-nine legions of spirits and depending on the number in a legion may be a number of approximately one hundred and fifty million. The first magick you will learn that uses Bethor is to be healed of all illness: and through this a longer life may also be bestowed. But you must will this magick to work so that it shall.

Bethor to be healed

Janus god of great power, you have two faces and while one of your faces always looks towards the future, one always looks towards the past. Janus, you control the gateway and I ask that you open the gates so that the way through to the Olympian spirits is open, the way through to the seven Alchemists. Janus open the gateway, open the gates here and now: Janus opens the gateway the gateway is open. Bethor second of the Olympian spirits, great alchemist, ruler of forty-two provinces, he of Jupiter and who may call on twenty-nine thousand legions of spirits. Bethor step through the gateway and be here with me: Bethor step through the gates and be here with me. Bethor step through the gates; Bethor steps through the gates and is here with me. Bethor, you are a greatly wise alchemist and healing and all magick are yours to control and I ask that you heal me of all illness so that long life and perfect health may be mine and this is what I ask of you. Bethor agrees to help and departs back through the gates. Janus god of great power, you have two faces and while one of your faces always looks towards the future, one always looks towards the past. Janus, you control the gateway and I ask that you close the gates. Janus close the gateway, close the gates here and now: Janus closes the gateway the gateway is shut. So it is and will be.

Here is some magick that is for you to be a powerful ruler and this is certainly a large thing to ask for. But Bethor has the power to grant this and so do use this magick. I feel that many people have been programmed to push power away when it comes and this is the exact reverse of what they should be doing. Embrace the way of power and you will find that it will help you: power has a way

of doing that when you have it. This magick I present here now for

you to use.

Bethor to be a powerful ruler

Janus god of great power, you have two faces and while one of

your faces always looks towards the future, one always looks

towards the past. Janus, you control the gateway and I ask that you

open the gates so that the way through to the Olympian spirits is

open, the way through to the seven Alchemists. Janus open the

gateway, open the gates here and now: Janus opens the gateway

the gateway is open. Bethor, second of the Olympian spirits, great

alchemist, ruler of forty-two provinces, he of Jupiter and who may

call on twenty-nine thousand legions of spirits. Bethor step through

the gateway and be here with me: Bethor step through the gates

and be here with me. Bethor step through the gates; Bethor steps

through the gates and is here with me. Bethor, you are a greatly

wise alchemist and healing and all magick are yours to control and

I ask that you make me a powerful ruler, so that great riches and

power shall be mine and this is what I ask of you. Bethor agrees to help and departs back through the gates. Janus god of great power, you have two faces and while one of your faces always looks towards the future, one always looks towards the past. Janus, you control the gateway and I ask that you close the gates. Janus close the gateway, close the gates here and now: Janus closes the gateway the gateway is shut. So it is and will be.

This next magick is simply for power and not to be a leader and this means that you will get assistance to get what sort of power is nearest. This means that for some people this may mean gaining more physical strength, for others a promotion but the power you gain will help you: and help you get more. It is easiest to gain power when we already have it and this means that this next magick will assist the last one and the last magick that next: basically, use them both. In fact, you may use all of the magick here and this will certainly help you gain a better life.

Bethor to be more powerful

Janus god of great power, you have two faces and while one of your faces always looks towards the future, one always looks towards the past. Janus, you control the gateway and I ask that you open the gates so that the way through to the Olympian spirits is open, the way through to the seven Alchemists. Janus open the gateway, open the gates here and now: Janus opens the gateway the gateway is open. Bethor second of the Olympian spirits, great alchemist, ruler of forty-two provinces, he of Jupiter and who may call on twenty-nine thousand legions of spirits. Bethor step through the gateway and be here with me: Bethor step through the gates and be here with me. Bethor step through the gates; Bethor steps through the gates and is here with me. Bethor, you are a greatly wise alchemist and healing and all magick are yours to control and I ask that you make me more powerful, make great power mine and this is what I ask of you. Bethor agrees to help and departs back through the gates. Janus god of great power, you have two faces and while one of your faces always looks towards the future, one always looks towards the past. Janus, you control the gateway and I ask that you close the gates. Janus close the gateway, close the gates here and now: Janus closes the gateway the gateway is shut. So it is and will be.

Here is some magick that is for great riches: for you to be rich. I know that many people forget that wealth is not opposite to occultism and there have been many rich occultists: Nicholas Flamel being one, and of course Abraham of Worms: he who wrote Abremlin the mage and also many bishops of the past that practiced occultism without telling anyone all while the Spanish inquisition was going on, and of course other periods. But here is magick to become richer: for great riches to be yours.

Bethor for great riches

Janus god of great power, you have two faces and while one of your faces always looks towards the future, one always looks towards the past. Janus, you control the gateway and I ask that you open the gates so that the way through to the Olympian spirits is open, the way through to the seven Alchemists. Janus open the gateway, open the gates here and now: Janus opens the gateway the gateway is open. Bethor second of the Olympian spirits, great alchemist, ruler of forty-two provinces, he of Jupiter and who may call on twenty-nine thousand legions of spirits. Bethor step through the gateway and be here with me: Bethor step through the gates and be here with me. Bethor step through the gates; Bethor steps through the gates and is here with me. Bethor, you are a greatly wise alchemist and healing and all magick are yours to control and I ask that you give me great riches, make great wealth mine and this is what I ask of you. Bethor agrees to help and departs back through the gates. Janus god of great power, you have two faces and while one of your faces always looks towards the future, one always looks towards the past. Janus, you control the gateway and I ask that you close the gates. Janus close the gateway, close the gates here and now: Janus closes the gateway the gateway is shut. So it is and will be.

I like to think that the Olympian spirits are a lot like us, and I feel that I many ways they are just overachievers and we should be inspired by them and certainly not scared of them. I feel they are here to help us out, to help maintain freewill and help all of creation to keep going. I feel for some reason that there is something of them within us and of this we should be proud.

Chapter 3

Phaleg is of Mars: he is linked that the planet Mars: and he is a war god, a great warrior as well as being an alchemist. Phaleg rules forty-two provinces and is a quite unusual Olympian Spirit because essentially to Phaleg, war is more important than magick: although this is his power. To Phaleg magick is a way to gain power and to win wars and this means that this magick that follows for Phaleg to be used to gain power will mean that this effect of the magick will have a ruthless edge to it. But this magick will work and here it is; will it to work and it shall.

Phaleg for power

Janus god of great power, you have two faces and while one of your faces always looks towards the future, one always looks towards the past. Janus, you control the gateway and I ask that you open the gates so that the way through to the Olympian spirits is open, the way through to the seven Alchemists. Janus open the gateway, open the gates here and now: Janus opens the gateway the gateway is open. Phaleg, third of the Olympian spirits, great alchemist, god of war, ruler of forty-two provinces, he of Mars. Phaleg step through the gateway and be here with me: Phaleg step through the gates and be here with me. Phaleg step through the gates; Phaleg steps through the gates and is here with me. Phaleg you are a great alchemist and warrior and fighting, war, protecting and all magick are yours to control and I ask that you make me more powerful and this is what I ask of you. Phaleg agrees to help and departs back through the gates. Janus god of great power, you have two faces and while one of your faces always looks towards the future, one always looks towards the past. Janus, you control the gateway and I ask that you close the gates. Janus close the gateway, close the gates here and now: Janus closes the gateway the gateway is shut. So it is and will be.

We all have enemies and we all need to be victorious over them and so do use this next magick. This magick will help you because we all have enemies whether we like it or not. But I think you should give Phaleg a try because if he was a human and not a magical being he would be the kind of homicidal genius that would be a great conversationalist in the pub. He is one of the Seven

Olympic Spirits and so no matter how odd or freakish you have ever felt you are like him and be will embrace you. Here is magick to be victorious over all enemies: use it and crush them.

Phaleg to be victorious over all enemies

Janus god of great power, you have two faces and while one of your faces always looks towards the future, one always looks towards the past. Janus, you control the gateway and I ask that you open the gates so that the way through to the Olympian spirits is open, the way through to the seven Alchemists. Janus open the gateway, open the gates here and now: Janus opens the gateway the gateway is open. Phaleg third of the Olympian spirits, great alchemist, god of war, ruler of forty-two provinces, he of Mars. Phaleg step through the gateway and be here with me: Phaleg step through the gates and be here with me. Phaleg step through the gates; Phaleg steps through the gates and is here with me. Phaleg, you are a great alchemist and warrior and fighting, war, protecting and all magick are yours to control and I ask that you help me become victorious over all enemies and this is what I ask of you. Phaleg agrees to help and departs back through the gates. Janus god of great power, you have two faces and while one of your faces always looks towards the future, one always looks towards the past. Janus, you control the gateway and I ask that you close the gates. Janus close the gateway, close the gates here and now: Janus closes the gateway the gateway is shut. So it is and will be.

If you want to be more successful then do use this next magick. Phaleg can help become more successful and this is not in any small part because he can be completely ruthless on your behalf. But also, he understands success because it is a lot like victory: success is often like winning a war in peace time. This magick is here to help, and so do use it and here it is ready and waiting for you to will it to work.

Phaleg for success

Janus god of great power, you have two faces and while one of your faces always looks towards the future, one always looks towards the past. Janus, you control the gateway and I ask that you open the gates so that the way through to the Olympian spirits is open, the way through to the seven Alchemists. Janus open the gateway, open the gates here and now: Janus opens the gateway the gateway is open. Phaleg third of the Olympian spirits, great alchemist, god of war, ruler of forty-two provinces, he of Mars. Phaleg step through the gateway and be here with me: Phaleg step through the gates and be here with me. Phaleg step through the gates; Phaleg steps through the gates and is here with me. Phaleg, you are a great alchemist and warrior and fighting, war, protecting and all magick are yours to control and I ask that you make me successful, give me great success of all types and this is what I ask of you. Phaleg agrees to help and departs back through the gates. Janus god of great power, you have two faces and while one of your faces always looks towards the future, one always looks towards the past. Janus, you control the gateway and I ask that you close the gates. Janus close the gateway, close the gates here and now: Janus closes the gateway the gateway is shut. So it is and will be.

Real estate is a form of wealth that makes a great deal of sense of Phaleg because this is the result of war in ancient times: land and property. But many people desire real estate and if this is you, then do use this magick here and now. Make a great amount of real estate yours and you will find yourself very powerful and very wealthy; and if you gain complete control over enough you may call yourself a king or queen and be quite correct to do so.

Phaleg to own a great amount of real estate

Janus god of great power, you have two faces and while one of your faces always looks towards the future, one always looks towards the past. Janus, you control the gateway and I ask that you open the gates so that the way through to the Olympian spirits is open, the way through to the seven Alchemists. Janus open the gateway, open the gates here and now: Janus opens the gateway the gateway is open. Phaleg third of the Olympian spirits, great alchemist, god of war, ruler of forty-two provinces, he of Mars. Phaleg step through the gateway and be here with me: Phaleg step through the gates and be here with me. Phaleg step through the gates; Phaleg steps through the gates and is here with me. Phaleg, you are a great alchemist and warrior and fighting, war, protecting and all magick are yours to control and I ask that you give me a great amount of real estate, make lots of property mine and this is what I ask of you. Phaleg agrees to help and departs back through the gates. Janus god of great power, you have two faces and while one of your faces always looks towards the future, one always looks towards the past. Janus, you control the gateway and I ask that you close the gates. Janus close the gateway, close the gates here and now: Janus closes the gateway the gateway is shut. So it is and will be.

I know that for many this chapter will have revealed a side to the world that was always in place to see and yet was unseen by them. In life it is often the case that life reveals to us what we would not have seen without some external force. But in this case, it is a person: myself S Rob: that has revealed this to you and having done so, you are at an advantage when compared to those that do not know this. Phaleg is easy to see in terms of how the world is partly him and we are also partly him. But it is he that gives us victory against difficulties he is for the bad and the good and like us he is powerful.

Chapter 4

Och is the fourth of the Olympian spirits and he is an alchemist, mage and physician. Och rules twenty-eight provinces and he is linked to the sun. The magick you will learn using Och first is for greater strength, and not just is his power about transformation and all magick but also about healing and so in a way strength covers all of these areas. But you must perform this magick with a strong will so that it will work: and this magick follows now.

Och for greater strength

Janus god of great power, you have two faces and while one of your faces always looks towards the future, one always looks towards the past. Janus, you control the gateway and I ask that you open the gates so that the way through to the Olympian Spirits is open, the way through to the seven Alchemists. Janus open the gateway, open the gates here and now: Janus opens the gateway the gateway is open. Och, fourth of the Olympian spirits, great alchemist, physician, mage, ruler of twenty-eight provinces, he of the Sun. Och step through the gateway and be here with me: Och step through the gates and be here with me. Och step through the gates; Och steps through the gates and is here with me. Och, you are a great, alchemist and physician, great mage, all magick is yours to control and I ask that you make me stronger in all ways and this is what I ask of you. Och agrees to help and departs back through the gates. Janus god of great power, you have two faces and while one of your faces always looks towards the future, one always looks towards the past. Janus, you control the gateway and I ask that you close the gates. Janus close the gateway, close the gates here and now: Janus closes the gateway the gateway is shut. So it is and will be.

If you wish to be more physically attractive then do use this next magick. In fact, the truth is that whatever anyone says, physical attractiveness is always an advantage. This magick is here to be used, and so do use it and help yourself. However, this magick often has a greater impact on how others see you, rather than you yourself: but this is what beauty really is.

Och to be more handsome and beautiful

Janus god of great power, you have two faces and while one of your faces always looks towards the future, one always looks towards the past. Janus, you control the gateway and I ask that you open the gates so that the way through to the Olympian spirits is open, the way through to the seven Alchemists. Janus open the gateway, open the gates here and now: Janus opens the gateway the gateway is open. Och, fourth of the Olympian spirits, great alchemist, physician, mage, ruler of twenty-eight provinces, he of the Sun. Och step through the gateway and be here with me: Och step through the gates and be here with me. Och step through the gates; Och steps through the gates and is here with me. Och, you are a great alchemist and physician, great mage, all magick is yours to control and I ask that you make me more beautiful and more handsome and this is what I ask of you. Och agrees to help and departs back through the gates. Janus god of great power, you have two faces and while one of your faces always looks towards the future, one always looks towards the past. Janus, you control the gateway and I ask that you close the gates. Janus close the gateway, close the gates here and now: Janus closes the gateway the gateway is shut. So it is and will be.

Great wealth is much better than no wealth; it is a lot better. Many people will seek the flaws of the person that is rich and blame the money when it is the person. The magick that follows will make you wealthier than you were: if you let it by performing it. Use your mind and will to reach out and command Och to make you richer, because this is what you do when you say these words that follow.

Och for greater wealth

Janus god of great power, you have two faces and while one of your faces always looks towards the future, one always looks towards the past. Janus, you control the gateway and I ask that you open the gates so that the way through to the Olympian spirits is open, the way through to the seven Alchemists. Janus open the gateway, open the gates here and now: Janus opens the gateway the gateway is open. Och, fourth of the Olympian spirits, great alchemist, physician, mage, ruler of twenty-eight provinces, he of the Sun. Och step through the gateway and be here with me: Och step through the gates and be here with me. Och step through the gates; Och steps through the gates and is here with me. Och you are a great, alchemist and physician, great mage, all magick is yours to control and I ask that you make me richer, make great riches mine and this is what I ask of you. Och agrees to help and departs back through the gates. Janus god of great power, you have two faces and while one of your faces always looks towards the future, one always looks towards the past. Janus, you control the gateway and I ask that you close the gates. Janus close the gateway, close the gates here and now: Janus closes the gateway the gateway is shut. So it is and will be.

Few if ever get through this world unharmed and this being the case this magick will be especially helpful. But I am not saying that you should not get whatever help medicine can for your problems, no I am saying this exists too to be used alongside this. But I also know that for some people medicine holds no solution and so for these people too this magick is here to help. Be healed but realise that healing is as diverse as the person because we all have many different types of wounds and problems: but this magick is helpful and here it is.

Och for healing

Janus god of great power, you have two faces and while one of your faces always looks towards the future, one always looks towards the past. Janus, you control the gateway and I ask that you open the gates so that the way through to the Olympian spirits is open, the way through to the seven Alchemists. Janus open the gateway, open the gates here and now: Janus opens the gateway the gateway is open. Och, fourth of the Olympian spirits, great alchemist, physician, mage, ruler of twenty-eight provinces, he of the Sun. Och step through the gateway and be here with me: Och step through the gates and be here with me. Och step through the gates; Och steps through the gates and is here with me. Och you are a great, alchemist and physician, great mage, all magick is yours to control and I ask that you heal me, heal me of all problems and illness and this is what I ask of you. Och agrees to help and departs back through the gates. Janus god of great power, you have two faces and while one of your faces always looks towards the future, one always looks towards the past. Janus, you control the gateway and I ask that you close the gates. Janus close the gateway, close the gates here and now: Janus closes the gateway the gateway is shut. So it is and will be.

You have gained a knowledge and insight into one more of the Seven Olympian Spirits. But I also hope that you realise that what is here is helpful and so a useful part of the world and your life. I know that magick that is useful is more likely to be used than that which is not. However, these entities are real and help us to understand that reality and even thought itself has many levels and is diverse. To only think that what we see is all that there is, is incorrect: but a choice many make. Reality is different to how you imagined, but this only reveals the power you can have if you embrace magick.

Chapter 5

Hagith is one of the Olympian spirits and he is linked with beauty and transmutation, magick and alchemy and of course the planet Venus. In fact, the ability to transmute: change things: is important because after all, these entities are also named the Seven Alchemists: all of them being alchemists. However, this magick here is useful to us in many ways because Hagith has power over magick and is very powerful; being able to command four thousand legions of spirits. The next magick is for great wealth: for you to be wealthier: use this magick and you will find that it works.

Hagith for great wealth

Janus god of great power, you have two faces and while one of your faces always looks towards the future, one always looks towards the past. Janus, you control the gateway and I ask that you open the gates so that the way through to the Olympian spirits is open, the way through to the seven Alchemists. Janus open the gateway, open the gates here and now: Janus opens the gateway the gateway is open. Hagith, fifth of the Olympian spirits, great alchemist, mage, ruler of twenty-one provinces, commander of four thousand legions of spirits, he of Venus. Hagith step through the gateway and be here with me: Hagith step through the gates and be here with me. Hagith step through the gates; Hagith steps through the gates and is here with me. Hagith you are a great, alchemist and great mage, all magick is yours to control and I ask that you send me great wealth, make me wealthy and this is what I ask of you. Hagith agrees to help and departs back through the gates. Janus god of great power, you have two faces and while one of your faces always looks towards the future, one always looks towards the past. Janus, you control the gateway and I ask that you close the gates. Janus close the gateway, close the gates here and now: Janus closes the gateway the gateway is shut. So it is and will be.

To be powerful is better than being powerless and so more power is good: if we agree on this then this next magick will be useful to you. I want you to be more powerful because if we are to look at the world, those with the most power and not doing a very good job. The world needs change and so be that change by working this magick and doing whatever else you need do to gain great power.

Hagith to be very powerful

Janus god of great power, you have two faces and while one of your faces always looks towards the future, one always looks towards the past. Janus, you control the gateway and I ask that you open the gates so that the way through to the Olympian spirits is open, the way through to the seven Alchemists. Janus open the gateway, open the gates here and now: Janus opens the gateway the gateway is open. Hagith, fifth of the Olympian spirits, great alchemist, mage, ruler of twenty-one provinces, commander of four thousand legions of spirits, he of Venus. Hagith step through the gateway and be here with me: Hagith step through the gates and be here with me. Hagith step through the gates; Hagith steps through the gates and is here with me. Hagith you are a great, alchemist and great mage, all magick is yours to control and I ask that you make me powerful, make great power mine and this is what I ask of you. Hagith agrees to help and departs back through the gates. Janus god of great power, you have two faces and while one of your faces always looks towards the future, one always looks towards the past. Janus, you control the gateway and I ask that you close the gates. Janus close the gateway, close the gates here and now: Janus closes the gateway the gateway is shut. So it is and will be.

The magick that follows now is to attract sex to you: so that you will have an abundance of sexual partners or at least for sex to be available whenever you desire. This makes this magick a good way to make your life better. Do use this magick so that it will work: because magick that is not performed at all will not do anything. Be the mage within by using this magick.

Hagith to attract sex

Janus god of great power, you have two faces and while one of your faces always looks towards the future, one always looks towards the past. Janus, you control the gateway and I ask that you open the gates so that the way through to the Olympian spirits is open, the way through to the seven Alchemists. Janus open the gateway, open the gates here and now: Janus opens the gateway the gateway is open. Hagith, fifth of the Olympian spirits, great

33

alchemist, mage, ruler of twenty-one provinces, commander of four thousand legions of spirits, he of Venus. Hagith step through the gateway and be here with me: Hagith step through the gates and be here with me. Hagith step through the gates; Hagith steps through the gates and is here with me. Hagith you are a great alchemist and great mage, all magick is yours to control and I ask that you attract sex to me, make sex mine in abundance and this is what I ask of you. Hagith agrees to help and departs back through the gates. Janus god of great power, you have two faces and while one of your faces always looks towards the future, one always looks towards the past. Janus, you control the gateway and I ask that you close the gates. Janus close the gateway, close the gates here and now: Janus closes the gateway the gateway is shut. So it is and will be.

This magick that follows is for you to have greater strength. Strength is sometimes a maligned trait; this makes little sense when we consider that this is a trait that makes our lives better. Use the magick that follows because the strength you gain: however, much that is: will only improve your life.

Hagith for great strength

Janus god of great power, you have two faces and while one of your faces always looks towards the future, one always looks towards the past. Janus, you control the gateway and I ask that you open the gates so that the way through to the Olympian spirits is open, the way through to the seven Alchemists. Janus open the gateway, open the gates here and now: Janus opens the gateway the gateway is open. Hagith, fifth of the Olympian spirits, great alchemist, mage, ruler of twenty-one provinces, commander of four thousand legions of spirits, he of Venus. Hagith step through the gateway and be here with me: Hagith step through the gates and be here with me. Hagith step through the gates; Hagith steps through the gates and is here with me. Hagith you are a great, alchemist and great mage, all magick is yours to control and I ask that you transform me so that I am stronger so that great strength is mine and this is what I ask of you. Hagith agrees to help and departs back through the gates. Janus god of great power, you have two faces and while one of your faces always looks towards the future, one always looks towards the past. Janus, you control the

35

gateway and I ask that you close the gates. Janus close the gateway, close the gates here and now: Janus closes the gateway the gateway is shut. So it is and will be.

You have progressed in knowledge and power although wisdom often flows from us: but not always. The fact is that magick improves lives, it makes things better through the power it gives. In many ways magick is like a swiss army penknife: it is ultra-adaptable and has many uses. However, the penknife itself will do nothing without the effort from us: which in magick comes in the form of our will. Just as the person must hold the penknife and take control and do something with it, so we must be prepared to take control of magick and do something with that: even when magick is represented by the Seven Olympian Spirits. Whatever form we take in our lives and whatever we must do we should always be prepared to act. In fact, when we do magick even when we look like we are doing nothing we rarely are: we are in fact doing something but not something easily viewed from this reality.

Chapter 6

You will now learn how to summon and use Ophiel for magick. Ophiel is an alchemist and is one of the greatest because those with his character, have the ability to create the philosophers stone: and this means that some people have spent their whole lives trying to be more like him. Ophiel is linked to the planet Mercury, and also art and all magick. Ophiel rules fourteen provinces and can command one hundred legions of spirits. The first magick you will learn using Ophiel is for great power: and here it is.

Ophiel for great power

Janus god of great power, you have two faces and while one of your faces always looks towards the future, one always looks towards the past. Janus, you control the gateway and I ask that you open the gates so that the way through to the Olympian spirits is open, the way through to the seven Alchemists. Janus open the gateway, open the gates here and now: Janus opens the gateway the gateway is open. Ophiel, sixth of the Olympian spirits, great alchemist, mage, ruler of fourteen provinces, commander of one

hundred thousand legions of spirits, he of the planet Mercury.
Ophiel step through the gateway and be here with me: Ophiel step
through the gates and be here with me. Ophiel step through the
gates; Ophiel steps through the gates and is here with me. Ophiel
you are a great alchemist and great mage, all magick is yours to
control and I ask that you make me more powerful, make great
power mine and this is what I ask of you. Ophiel agrees to help and
departs back through the gates. Janus god of great power, you have
two faces and while one of your faces always looks towards the
future, one always looks towards the past. Janus, you control the
gateway and I ask that you close the gates. Janus close the
gateway, close the gates here and now: Janus closes the gateway
the gateway is shut. So it is and will be.

Here is some magick that will increase your artistic talents and this
magick certainly is useful. In fact, creativity and a greater artistic
talent gives to us a mental adaptability that we otherwise would not
have. But this magick will help you gain a greater artistic talent but
you still must practice: will this magick to work and it shall.

Ophiel for great artistic talent

Janus god of great power, you have two faces and while one of your faces always looks towards the future, one always looks towards the past. Janus, you control the gateway and I ask that you open the gates so that the way through to the Olympian spirits is open, the way through to the seven Alchemists. Janus open the gateway, open the gates here and now: Janus opens the gateway the gateway is open. Ophiel, sixth of the Olympian spirits, great alchemist, mage, ruler of fourteen provinces, commander of one hundred thousand legions of spirits, he of the planet Mercury. Ophiel step through the gateway and be here with me: Ophiel step through the gates and be here with me. Ophiel step through the gates; Ophiel steps through the gates and is here with me. Ophiel you are a great alchemist and great mage, all magick is yours to control and I ask that you give me great artistic talent and this is what I ask of you. Ophiel agrees to help and departs back through the gates. Janus god of great power, you have two faces and while one of your faces always looks towards the future, one always looks towards the past. Janus, you control the gateway and I ask that you close the gates. Janus close the gateway, close the gates here and now: Janus closes the gateway the gateway is shut. So it is and will be.

Ophiel being a very great alchemist and mage, can give you hidden knowledge. But do bear in mind that often this is done through a series of clues and perhaps even examples. But do use this magick, it will help you to understand all that is hidden in this world and others. I know that there is more hidden in this world that that which is not. Use this magick and be enlightened.

Ophiel for hidden knowledge

Janus god of great power, you have two faces and while one of your faces always looks towards the future, one always looks towards the past. Janus, you control the gateway and I ask that you open the gates so that the way through to the Olympian spirits is open, the way through to the seven Alchemists. Janus open the gateway, open the gates here and now: Janus opens the gateway the gateway is open. Ophiel, sixth of the Olympian spirits, great alchemist, mage, ruler of fourteen provinces, commander of one hundred thousand legions of spirits, he of the planet Mercury.

Ophiel step through the gateway and be here with me: Ophiel step through the gates and be here with me. Ophiel step through the gates; Ophiel steps through the gates and is here with me. Ophiel you are a great alchemist and great mage, all magick is yours to control and I ask that you give me hidden knowledge, let me know the knowledge that is hidden from common view and this is what I ask of you. Ophiel agrees to help and departs back through the gates. Janus god of great power, you have two faces and while one of your faces always looks towards the future, one always looks towards the past. Janus, you control the gateway and I ask that you close the gates. Janus close the gateway, close the gates here and now: Janus closes the gateway the gateway is shut. So it is and will be.

The magick that follows can attract wealth to you: in fact, the getting of wealth often required not just magick, but it does help. Use this magick because by doing so you can only gain, you will lose nothing. Magick is here to help you and this is done through the use of magick: you need to help yourself by willing what is here to work. This magick is tremendous and here it is.

Ophiel for great wealth

Janus god of great power, you have two faces and while one of your faces always looks towards the future, one always looks towards the past. Janus, you control the gateway and I ask that you open the gates so that the way through to the Olympian spirits is open, the way through to the seven Alchemists. Janus open the gateway, open the gates here and now: Janus opens the gateway the gateway is open. Ophiel, sixth of the Olympian spirits, great alchemist, mage, ruler of fourteen provinces, commander of one hundred thousand legions of spirits, he of the planet Mercury. Ophiel step through the gateway and be here with me: Ophiel step through the gates and be here with me. Ophiel step through the gates; Ophiel steps through the gates and is here with me. Ophiel you are a great alchemist and great mage, all magick is yours to control and I ask that you give me great riches, make me wealthy and this is what I ask of you. Ophiel agrees to help and departs back through the gates. Janus god of great power, you have two faces and while one of your faces always looks towards the future, one always looks towards the past. Janus, you control the gateway and I ask that you close the gates. Janus close the gateway, close the gates here and now: Janus closes the gateway the gateway is shut. So it is and will be.

I want you to transform your life through what is here. There is no reason why your life cannot be made better because you have real magick working for you. You should expect magick to help you: this is not an irrational expectation. But to do this you need to work magick that is for you to gain something, and perform that magick with a strong will. As in many things in life, it is made better for you often by yourself. This means that I want you to look for the opportunities and other help this magick gives and to embrace that which you think is helpful and what you want. But this is a choice and you can if you choose use this magick and do nothing more, and perhaps even pull back from the positive effects of this magick. Magick is also a choice and we could choose not to use magick and not to get its benefit. However, if we were to make this choice we need to remember that this does not stop others from getting its benefits: meaning you would be putting yourself as a relative disadvantage: magick is to be used.

Chapter 7

Phul is Lord of the powers of the Moon and Supreme Lord of the Waters, he is a strong and powerful mage. The first magick here is for you to have a longer life, and this is important because why not live a long and healthy life? But also, this magick is a way of you getting to know Phul and this is important too. In time I feel that many people get a feeling for these spirits even so much that they can assign a personality to them. But do use this magick so that it may help you.

Phul for a long life

Janus god of great power, you have two faces and while one of your faces always looks towards the future, one always looks towards the past. Janus, you control the gateway and I ask that you open the gates so that the way through to the Olympian spirits is open, the way through to the seven Alchemists. Janus open the gateway, open the gates here and now: Janus opens the gateway the gateway is open. Phul, seventh of the Olympian spirits, great alchemist, mage, Lord of the powers of the Moon, Supreme Lord of the waters, ruler of seven provinces, he of the Moon. Phul step through the gateway and be here with me: Phul step through the gates and be here with me. Phul step through the gates; Phul steps through the gates and is here with me. Phul you are a great alchemist and great mage, all magick is yours to control and I ask that you give me a long life, let me be healthy and live a long time and this is what I ask of you. Phul agrees to help and departs back through the gates. Janus god of great power, you have two faces and while one of your faces always looks towards the future, one always looks towards the past. Janus, you control the gateway and I ask that you close the gates. Janus close the gateway, close the gates here and now: Janus closes the gateway the gateway is shut. So it is and will be.

Success is the result of this magick and this is not one type of success but success generally. This means that this next magick will be greatly helpful because after all, success generally is like a rising tide that raises all boats: meaning it affects all aspects of your life positively. So reach out to Phul so that he may help you.

Phul for success

Janus god of great power, you have two faces and while one of your faces always looks towards the future, one always looks towards the past. Janus, you control the gateway and I ask that you open the gates so that the way through to the Olympian spirits is open, the way through to the seven Alchemists. Janus open the gateway, open the gates here and now: Janus opens the gateway the gateway is open. Phul, seventh of the Olympian spirits, great alchemist, mage, Lord of the powers of the Moon, Supreme Lord of the waters, ruler of seven provinces, he of the Moon. Phul step through the gateway and be here with me: Phul step through the gates and be here with me. Phul step through the gates; Phul steps through the gates and is here with me. Phul you are a great alchemist and great mage, all magick is yours to control and I ask that you make me a success, give great success to me and this is what I ask of you. Phul agrees to help and departs back through the gates. Janus god of great power, you have two faces and while one of your faces always looks towards the future, one always looks towards the past. Janus, you control the gateway and I ask that you close the gates. Janus close the gateway, close the gates here and now: Janus closes the gateway the gateway is shut. So it is and will be.

If you desire to be a great leader then do use this magick that follows. This magick is fantastic to use because being a leader gives great power. In fact, many of the things that people want, they will get if they are a great leader. But you must also embrace the leadership ability within yourself, you need to do this so that your life will be transformed and through it you may also transform the world.

Phul to be a great leader

Janus god of great power, you have two faces and while one of your faces always looks towards the future, one always looks towards the past. Janus, you control the gateway and I ask that you open the gates so that the way through to the Olympian spirits is open, the way through to the seven Alchemists. Janus open the gateway, open the gates here and now: Janus opens the gateway the gateway is open. Phul, seventh of the Olympian spirits, great alchemist, mage, Lord of the powers of the Moon, Supreme Lord of the waters, ruler of seven provinces, he of the Moon. Phul step through the gateway and be here with me: Phul step through the gates and be here with me. Phul step through the gates; Phul steps through the gates and is here with me. Phul you are a great alchemist and great mage, all magick is yours to control and I ask that you make me a great and powerful leader and this is what I ask of you. Phul agrees to help and departs back through the gates. Janus god of great power, you have two faces and while one of your faces always looks towards the future, one always looks towards the past. Janus, you control the gateway and I ask that you close the gates. Janus close the gateway, close the gates here and now: Janus closes the gateway the gateway is shut. So it is and will be.

Use this magick and have greater wealth; this magick is to do this. However, you must perform the ritual while really willing magick to be worked: and done so with a strong will. But in fact, wealth is an easily converted form of power: it is easily transformed from one form into another. This means that wealth has many benefits outside of those expected: use this magick and become richer and quite possibly rich. But do realise that what you do with this wealth is for you to decide and if you make mistakes with it and let it amplify your negative qualities and they work against you, then that is down to you and not the wealth. I fact many people use wealth to make them stronger and to improve their lives and even the world.

Phul for greater wealth

Janus god of great power, you have two faces and while one of your faces always looks towards the future, one always looks towards the past. Janus, you control the gateway and I ask that you open the gates so that the way through to the Olympian spirits is open, the way through to the seven Alchemists. Janus open the gateway, open the gates here and now: Janus opens the gateway the gateway is open. Phul, seventh of the Olympian spirits, great alchemist, mage, Lord of the powers of the Moon, Supreme Lord of the waters, ruler of seven provinces, he of the Moon. Phul step through the gateway and be here with me: Phul step through the gates and be here with me. Phul step through the gates; Phul steps through the gates and is here with me. Phul you are a great alchemist and great mage, all magick is yours to control and I ask that you give me great wealth, make greater wealth mine and this is what I ask of you. Phul agrees to help and departs back through the gates. Janus god of great power, you have two faces and while one of your faces always looks towards the future, one always looks towards the past. Janus, you control the gateway and I ask that you close the gates. Janus close the gateway, close the gates here and now: Janus closes the gateway the gateway is shut. So it is and will be.

This chapter has given you more of an insight into the hidden world that is the Seven Olympic Spirits. You have now learnt to use all seven of these spirits for real magick and this is no small feat. But if you thought this magick has finished you were wrong, there is more to follow. However, all that you have learnt is useful and important, your skills and powers will have increased along with your insight. You may look the same to the world but only because they do not have your insight, because you know more than you did and can see past the hidden veil and see what is really behind it.

Chapter 8

The magick in this chapter will use all Seven Olympian Spirits together, and this does mean that you should have used some magick with each and even one of these spirits individually. This magick is here to help you: but it does require a strong will. However other than that this magick is quite easy and here it is: magick for great power.

Seven Olympian Spirits for great power

Janus god of great power, you have two faces and while one of your faces always looks towards the future, one always looks towards the past. Janus, you control the gateway and I ask that you open the gates so that the way through to the Olympian spirits is open, the way through to the seven Alchemists. Janus open the gateway, open the gates here and now: Janus opens the gateway the gateway is open. Aratron first of the Olympian spirits, great alchemist, ruler of forty-nine provinces, he of Saturn and who may call on seventeen million six hundred and forty thousand spirits. Aratron step through the gateway and be here with me: Aratron step through the gates and be here with me. Aratron step through the gates; Aratron steps through the gates and is here with me. Bethor second of the Olympian spirits, great alchemist, ruler of forty-two provinces, he of Jupiter and who may call on twenty-nine thousand legions of spirits. Bethor step through the gateway and be here with me: Bethor step through the gates and be here with me. Bethor step through the gates; Bethor steps through the gates and is here with me. Phaleg, third of the Olympian spirits, great alchemist, god of war, ruler of forty-two provinces, he of Mars. Phaleg step through the gateway and be here with me: Phaleg step through the gates and be here with me. Phaleg step through the gates; Phaleg steps through the gates and is here with me. Och, fourth of the Olympian spirits, great alchemist, physician, mage, ruler of twenty-eight provinces, he of the Sun. Och step through the gateway and be here with me: Och step through the gates and be here with me. Och step through the gates; Och steps through the gates and is here with me. Hagith, fifth of the Olympian spirits, great alchemist, mage, ruler of twenty-one provinces, commander of four thousand legions of spirits, he of Venus. Hagith step through the gateway and be here with me:

Hagith step through the gates and be here with me. Hagith step through the gates; Hagith steps through the gates and is here with me. Ophiel, sixth of the Olympian spirits, great alchemist, mage, ruler of fourteen provinces, commander of one hundred thousand legions of spirits, he of the planet Mercury. Ophiel step through the gateway and be here with me: Ophiel step through the gates and be here with me. Ophiel step through the gates; Ophiel steps through the gates and is here with me. Phul, seventh of the Olympian spirits, great alchemist, mage, Lord of the powers of the Moon, Supreme Lord of the waters, ruler of seven provinces, he of the Moon. Phul step through the gateway and be here with me: Phul step through the gates and be here with me. Phul step through the gates; Phul steps through the gates and is here with me. Aratron you are a great alchemist and transformation and all magick are yours to control and I ask that you give me greater power, make greater power mine and this is what I ask of you. Bethor, you are a greatly wise alchemist and healing and all magick are yours to control and I ask that you give me greater power, make great power mine and this is what I ask of you. Phaleg you are a great alchemist and warrior and fighting, war, protecting and all magick are yours to control and I ask that you make me more powerful and this is what I ask of you. Och, you are a great, alchemist and physician, great mage, all magick is yours to control and I ask that you make me more powerful in all ways and this is what I ask of you. Hagith you are a great, alchemist and great mage, all magick is yours to control and I ask that you give me more power so that great power shall be mine and this is what I ask of you. Ophiel you are a great alchemist and great mage, all magick is yours to control and I ask that you make me more powerful, make great power mine and this is what I ask of you. Phul you are a great alchemist and great mage, all magick is yours to control and I ask that you give me the gift of power, make me greatly powerful and this is what I ask of you. Aratron agrees to help and departs back through the gates. Bethor agrees to help and departs back through the gates. Phaleg agrees to help and departs back through the gates. Och agrees to help and departs back through the gates. Hagith agrees to help and departs back through the gates. Ophiel agrees to help and departs back through the gates. Phul agrees to help and departs back through the gates. Janus god of great power, you have two faces and while one of your faces always looks towards the future, one always looks towards the past. Janus, you control the gateway and I ask that you close the gates. Janus close the gateway, close the gates here and now: Janus closes the gateway the gateway is shut. So it is and will be.

If you want to have great wealth then use this next magick. This magick does utilise all seven of the Olympian Spirits, and so as before you need to have performed some magick with each spirit individually. This magick is powerful and here it is for you to use: and get rich.

Seven Olympian Spirits for great wealth

Janus god of great power, you have two faces and while one of your faces always looks towards the future, one always looks towards the past. Janus, you control the gateway and I ask that you open the gates so that the way through to the Olympian spirits is open, the way through to the seven Alchemists. Janus open the gateway, open the gates here and now: Janus opens the gateway the gateway is open. Aratron first of the Olympian spirits, great alchemist, ruler of forty-nine provinces, he of Saturn and who may call on seventeen million six hundred and forty thousand spirits.

Aratron step through the gateway and be here with me: Aratron step through the gates and be here with me. Aratron step through the gates; Aratron steps through the gates and is here with me. Bethor second of the Olympian spirits, great alchemist, ruler of forty-two provinces, he of Jupiter and who may call on twenty-nine thousand legions of spirits. Bethor step through the gateway and be here with me: Bethor step through the gates and be here with me. Bethor step through the gates; Bethor steps through the gates and is here with me. Phaleg, third of the Olympian spirits, great alchemist, god of war, ruler of forty-two provinces, he of Mars. Phaleg step through the gateway and be here with me: Phaleg step through the gates and be here with me. Phaleg step through the gates; Phaleg steps through the gates and is here with me. Och, fourth of the Olympian spirits, great alchemist, physician, mage, ruler of twenty-eight provinces, he of the Sun. Och step through the gateway and be here with me: Och step through the gates and be here with me. Och step through the gates; Och steps through the gates and is here with me. Hagith, fifth of the Olympian spirits, great alchemist, mage, ruler of twenty-one provinces, commander of four thousand legions of spirits, he of

Venus. Hagith step through the gateway and be here with me: Hagith step through the gates and be here with me. Hagith step through the gates; Hagith steps through the gates and is here with me. Ophiel, sixth of the Olympian spirits, great alchemist, mage, ruler of fourteen provinces, commander of one hundred thousand legions of spirits, he of the planet Mercury. Ophiel step through the gateway and be here with me: Ophiel step through the gates and be here with me. Ophiel step through the gates; Ophiel steps through the gates and is here with me. Phul, seventh of the Olympian spirits, great alchemist, mage, Lord of the powers of the Moon, Supreme Lord of the waters, ruler of seven provinces, he of the Moon. Phul step through the gateway and be here with me: Phul step through the gates and be here with me. Phul step through the gates; Phul steps through the gates and is here with me. Aratron you are a great alchemist and transformation and all magick are yours to control and I ask that you give me greater wealth, make greater wealth mine and this is what I ask of you. Bethor, you are a greatly wise alchemist and healing and all magick are yours to control and I ask that you make wealth in all forms flow to me, make great riches mine and this is what I ask of you. Phaleg you

57

are a great alchemist and warrior and fighting, war, protecting and all magick are yours to control and I ask that you make me wealthier and this is what I ask of you. Och, you are a great, alchemist and physician, great mage, all magick is yours to control and I ask that you make me wealthy, let money and all types of wealth flow to me and this is what I ask of you. Hagith you are a great, alchemist and great mage, all magick is yours to control and I ask that you make wealth flow to me and this is what I ask of you. Ophiel you are a great alchemist and great mage, all magick is yours to control and I ask that you make me richer, make great wealth mine and this is what I ask of you. Phul you are a great alchemist and great mage, all magick is yours to control and I ask that you give me the gift of wealth, make me rich and this is what I ask of you. Aratron agrees to help and departs back through the gates. Bethor agrees to help and departs back through the gates. Phaleg agrees to help and departs back through the gates. Och agrees to help and departs back through the gates. Hagith agrees to help and departs back through the gates. Ophiel agrees to help and departs back through the gates. Phul agrees to help and departs back through the gates. Janus god of great power, you have two faces and while one of your faces always looks towards the future, one always looks towards the past. Janus, you control the gateway and I ask that you close the gates. Janus close the gateway, close the gates here and now: Janus closes the gateway the gateway is shut. So it is and will be.

The magick here is a part of you just as all knowledge gained becomes a part of us. Through this magick you have grown and so are more than you were. But do know that this magick will be yours to use whenever you want. This does mean that you should walk the Earth with a confident stride because you have a power working for you that others do not: your friends are the Seven Olympic Spirits, reality is yours to alter. You have gained power and now the world waits to see what you choose to do with it.

Made in the USA
Las Vegas, NV
20 March 2023